Mirrored Time

Elizabeth Barton

First published 2023 by The Hedgehog Poetry Press

Published in the UK by
The Hedgehog Poetry Press
Coppack House, 5
Churchill Avenue
Clevedon
BS21 6QW

www.hedgehogpress.co.uk

ISBN: 978-1-913499-68-6

Copyright © Elizabeth Barton 2023

The right of Elizabeth Barton to be identified as the author of this work has been asserted in accordance with the Copyright, Designs and Patents Act 1988.

All rights reserved. No part of this publication may be reproduced, stored in or introduced into a retrieval system, or transmitted in any form, or by any means (electronic, mechanical, photocopying, recording or otherwise) without prior written permissions of the publisher. Any person who does any unauthorised act in relation to this publication may be liable for criminal prosecution and civil claims for damages,

9 8 7 6 5 4 3 2 1

A CIP Catalogue record for this book is available from the British Library.

Contents

Mirrored Time 5
The Miner's Triumph 6
Uncertainty 8
Double Take 9
Eel Pie Island 10
The Dichotomy of Isis 11
The Long Good Night 12
Lunar Eclipse 13
Nightfall 14
A Christmas Voyage 15
Solaris 16
Venus Reluctantly 17
Happy Entrance 18
At the King's Head, Wye 19
The Moth 20
Pasiphae 21
Adonis 22
Judgment 23
Watchword 24
Released 25

MIRRORED TIME

Here come the clouds, devoutly wished for;
a soft grey duvet unrolls slowly
to beckon enchantment into the light,
a magic theatre mask drapes heaven
for the sky's blue face to slip behind.

I timed it right; I returned to a place
under a feathered overcast, remembered
in childhood dreams, a whispered past
sweeping me like stardust to the future.
The gift of irony fell under my gaze;

an iconic clock with backward hands winked
from the wall of a children's slide
as I wandered in a mirrored world, taking me
to the well of dreams, beyond life and death,
a reflected sphere in which one day, I may abide.

THE MINER'S TRIUMPH

Sometimes it's enough to read
the grain, cut to the face,
suffering in the cut, the search
with hands and heart softly trace
the arch and curve alive
in the darkness of the earth.

The cut is the feel of the path
overhung with age and veiled danger,
walled by doubt, hidden and strange
to feet embedding sod with courage;
cold air clung with gossamer threads
catch the gleam of a lonely star.

The disquieting moment descends
in the damp cathedral air
where darkness binds with uncertainty
and light is but a memory
held by diaphanous threads
in the dim cavern of hope.

Tapestries made by moonlight
dance in ghostly shapes
lace scintillate grey shadow
on streaming rock and hidden vein
remind me of a damp, cold cave
in which I found my wish.

I hope I never have to meet blind fate
or lose my strength and will to pass
deep night in a deathly stone embrace,
then to rise reborn in morning light
held like gold nuggets in my hand
the foundation stone of heart and land.

I hope I never have to shed vain tears
for pale regret or tame wild love,
let all flow in me as a gushing weir
where gold winks in rock and stream,
revere what stops my heart with joy
close in my clasp, with jubilant voice.

UNCERTAINTY

I become aware of the world about me,
the clang of chain on gate as a farmer
leaves his field; passing shadows of cows,
shifting light cast by meandering clouds;
the circling of stars taking new stations
as winter nips the air with crisp promise.

The world is slowing, flowing with centuries,
time treacles in a warmed pot mellowed
by the heat of otherworldly, unworldly changes;
breath is held in the slow gold simmering,
mixing anxiety and hope in tense alchemy,
a binding of spirit, a release of mind.

DOUBLE TAKE

My Muse tumbled me to the intrigue;
It was time to don my hat and leave,
Cast my lot in with Lot
With never a backward glance.

No salty pillar to etch my form
As on windward journey I hasten,
Not for me the wind to shake
My ashes high with heavy cloud,
To lose and be born as someone else.

Write a century's tale for someone else to tell;
A lie, some imagined fate, may wash the dreams
Of sleeping fools, and force their lips
As I wend my way, toward the dawn.

I am born of light, of wind on water,
The play of rain in leaves;
I'm the moment at the horizon before first light,
The purple line between dawn and land,
The song in the rising of the sun.

EEL PIE ISLAND

The Fisher King lives on Eel Pie Island;
the old man who serves you spell draughts and drinks
behind curtains of sleep does not mind
the flimsy rumours that fly with a blink
and circulate the late happy rounds;
he'll wink at you with a hooking clue,
start at the gem you have lately found.
You'll tremble at what you thought you knew
before time's winter swept wisdom away,
and you had to ask your way to the shore
of the strange Eel Pie Island arranged
in shadow and rough forested lore:
Fisherman, guide me on my blessed trip,
let me hold the sweet Grail to my parched lips.

THE DICHOTOMY OF ISIS

The god in his dream abides
cosseted in a lair of rejoicing;
we glimpse him in a breathless vision
and clasp our hands in euphoric worship,
though when he at last appears
we become careless and forget
the beauteous form which seized us
in thrall but a moment before.
The flesh is illusory, the veil unkind,
yet in the mundane features
sparks conspire to ignite the divine,
and recall the vision we had abandoned
like a cruel lover's rejecting hand
still tingling with the touch of our wish.

THE LONG GOOD NIGHT

Sinking into the long good night
Warmed by a lover's extravagant kiss,
His little words entice with promises
Neatly gifted like a velvet tomb,
A brevity of shadows wrap up life
To keep the prick of interest alive.

All the days of waiting for unwritten wishes
To find wing and unfold in vivid play,
That writhe and dance to a stale tune
Still gaze demurely at the empty sky.

A cave of echoes fills with slow goodbyes,
A wreath of broken hopes and flighty words
Threads like a shroud her pale visage
Searching in a vaulted sky;
Now trembling on a pillow of thorns
She sighs regrets to the long good night.

LUNAR ECLIPSE

July 2019

The Eclipse brought about a change of mind
In the blink of opposition conferred,
Currents of insight as shadows unwind
In the face of dark moon the old deferred.
Spectral cities fall in a liquid sky
Built with thoughts of ornately trite belief,
And so it seems they were all lovely lies
As I cast them aside with glad relief.
Trumpet the moon on her ascendancy
As she rises in the cloak of the sun;
Gold, like music, patterns her regency
As she holds sway in foolish forms undone;
A suffuse epiphany proves her art,
As from all I have known I now depart.

NIGHTFALL

Trees like lost cities pierce the skyline
tenebrous shadows evoke dream fragments;
time winds endlessly in the great orb of the sun,
days listlessly drawn with the weight of the past
descend into the fruitful womb of night
leaving old tales to drift on the wind.
Unthreaded memories lift on violet air
and wander, ancient pilgrims in happy throng,
voices through valleys echoed with their dead.
Trees nurse tattered myths in shadowy forms;
histories borne on the changing shapes of dusk
inhabit a realm of growing darkness;
epochs of journeys emerge on the wing
within the transiting space, pitch sky to earth,
girded with dreamscapes, the roving storm
flickering worlds behind the dreamer's eye.

A CHRISTMAS VOYAGE

The sea gloaming pale and turbulent
displays the white horses of Rhiannon
who will bear my lover to me,
manuka as white as the Lamb of God
spills an ocean of blooms, foaming
glorious, bridal as stars to shipwrecks;
the bursting flowers fecundly bright
weigh branches with their excessive seed,
a glacier of turgid ice holding a thousand years
in its patient, entombing embrace
recount the perennial manuka blooms
cascading wantonly at Christmas Eve,
drawing my lover to these shores
on waves of snow-capped seas.

SOLARIS

Imagine you had written a poem
That a hundred years from now
Was woven into a film.
The dying lovers reunited, recite
The talismanic verses in a pact,
And remember their lives in happier days,
Before sorrow laid thorns at their heads
And kismet crowned them with regrets.

A spaceship of arcane origin holds a secret
That may win them back their lives;
The poem placed in the immortal theme
Glows like a posy in a window.
Assembled frames mark the passing of days,
Film frames stitch a quilt of questions
Urged by the calling of obscure memories,
A rubric of time caught in a fragile maze.

Here is the rose of remembrance,
Furnished with dark petals a richer life,
Rounded in its joyous symmetry a chance
To take back what fate had lost.
At the root of all wandering the wider world
Lies recollection of exile; at the end
A blue jewel beholds an ancient poem
In which is revealed the end of death.

The lovers, by its covenant, joined in life
Wreathe the poem beyond the grave.
If I had authored such a poem
I would be quickened by prophetic fire;
I would come back at once from the dead,
Linger at the portals of life and death
Poised as a stranger on the threshold,
Enthralled by the film to hear the poem read.

VENUS RELUCTANTLY

Languishing, like Venus who had lost her memory,
With no Cupid adoring her, upholding a mirror,
Or winsome beau with scrutinizing brow
Bent forward, to shower her with favours,
She lingers on a couch of wondering,
She spends time in a forest of questions;
There is a map somewhere in wind-tossed leaves,
In slant of afternoon sun, that leads to a path,
The way out of a maze of uncertainty;
There is direction hinted at in time,
In the flicker of leaves in the light,
In the dance of shadows on the forest floor;
Cupid's arrow points assuringly, a beacon
In a wayward journey upon a restless sea,
And she might find her way home,
Discover lost Venus in her own reflection,
The way a star on water tremulously beckons,
The way night informs her what she has always known.

HAPPY ENTRANCE

Weakness tends upon my shoulder
like a fretting, solicitous aunt
worried about the noisy wind.

For fear of the deluge
my voice is diluted, lost flutes on air,
when I strode like Mars proudly.

Let the deluge come and howl,
let my voice sing like the tempest,
girded with strength, raise loudly.

The gates of heaven may break,
the gates of freedom fly open;
my charge is the happy entrance.

AT THE KING'S HEAD, WYE

Hang loose Western style
In the saddle of her braless comfort,
Emerald top conjures summer fields
Against the crowded lunchtime grey.

Gypsy slung to the moment,
Shy stranger in a hostile throng,
An unexpected sashay, hipster clung
On the gangway of unintended consequence.

Hapless portraits of men with guns
Cocked and splayed on the wall behind,
Chinless wonders strew dank fields
Find amusement on coppiced hills.

Hasten the pleasure of the play,
A joke that curves a clever smile,
The god of love droops his head
Arching Cupid's mocking bow.

Hunting hounds swarm the happy meadows
As men, like shadows, fall in behind,
Follow the chase with faces furrowed,
Trip on the quarry they hope to find.

THE MOTH

A cold unsolved murder haunts the headlines,
loose threads entangle a dapper stranger
who was dubbed the Moth, in a web entwined
his secret dalliance keyed with danger.
Notebooks found detailed a thousand women,
conquests worthy of a king, but not one
hand revealed the motive or cause of death,
just as the moth is silent, mostly shunned.
Bold, he scratched his yearnings on window panes,
announcing his amorous intrusion,
flitting shadow fevered with lusty gain,
like the moth, blinded by blazed illusion -
he had found his flame in a cruel axe blow,
the man who rapped love at women's windows.

PASIPHAE

Nerves of fire burn brightest with sharp lust;
Defiance of the heavenly order
Tempted her gaze, and scored the ground where dust
Flew in the gaping space peace lay before.
Turbulent longing forged her dark disguise;
Brutish trickster gods captured her in thrall
And in her possession, clouded her eye
As she claimed her prize under night's soft pall.
Neptune seized her as Aldebaran gazed,
The flickering white star returned her wish.
Her threaded life bore the workings of Fate
When sacrificial smoke hazed her last gift;
Into the night embers of virgins rose
Lighting the pyre only doomed lovers know.

ADONIS

He dreamed of himself – or who he thought he was.
His steps clipped a victory slut walk
through the streets of high dudgeon,
hung with fluttering shame in the market place
of closed minds and shuttered doors;
all he imagined on his tight rope,
preened and handsome for all the girls,
but nailed with his colours to Mummy's mast.

Good child, the future promised him,
to wed and follow the grating maxim;
Prometheus lies chained to the rock,
helpless in the eagle's glare –
the maxim with rivaled pecking insistence
drilled holes and left their bloody mark,
the brand of his mother's admonition:
'Cows and women from your own country.'

JUDGMENT

A black sun traces her firm mouth,
A vicious eclipse inscribing a taut visage;
The hellfire of judgment assaults her frame
And torments her mind to richly accuse
Innocent beauties who flower her path.

There is no wrath to match her own,
An original fanatic steeped in Inquisitor's ink;
She girds her announcements with edgy fire
To burn the goodness from all she sees,
To gain all power from a stolen throne.

Thinking God's blessings glint in her eye,
She does not know how she is misled
Or that perverse devilry loves her lies,
Or with mad fires her ramblings are fed
And forked phenomena shadow her steps
Lighting the air where devils fly.

That which is divinely compassed
Is for her the devil's work;
'Inspired by Satan,' she declares
To works of celestial signature.
The deceiving lure of infernal pacts
Dazzles fools with virtuous acts.

WATCHWORD

The watchword of Venus is cast on the ocean
Riding the wave of the magic syllable,
Building a rhythm at the shores of her temple
With moonlight jewelled on the undulating sea.

The mystery is in the lull of night air,
In the pause between the inward breath
And the sigh of the outgoing tide,
The swell of the deep rises in the lungs

Filling the throat with glorious voice,
Drawing down the spears of ageless stars
To strike the waves with shimmering light,
Dancing the weave of sinuous melodies.

The mythic script falls below the waterline
Where Neptune's playground once held sway,
Its cursive wave rolls in the architects' ruins,
Covert in the barnacles of watery graves.

RELEASED

I've broken through the hullabaloo,
the moon was never more mad
as she raced rose clouds in a smoky sky
and ran cold fingers over rushing rills,
speeding silver as deft as the gods' brisk
messenger assumes his secret toil;
I ran that river to the sea
and the gaping wet expanse clothes me,
blue as subdued victory, thick as night,
silent with all the hurrying stars.

ACKNOWLEDGEMENTS

The Miner's Triumph originally appeared in Vita Brevis Literature's E-Journal, with thanks to Brian Geiger, editor.

The Long Good Night, Venus Reluctantly and *Watchword* made their debut with the New York based e-zine, Spillwords.com, with much gratitude to Dagmara K., editor.

I would like to thank the editor of Hedgehog Poetry Press, Mark Davidson, for his tireless dedication to the Hedgehog Poetry experience and keeping the fires of poetry alive with his support and encouragement, and for publishing my collection *Mirrored Time*, which to my delight, was joint winner in the *White Label: Cinq* Competition 2020.